THE
BEST RECIPES
COSTA RICA

• Recipes and Food Styling: Tatiana Coto • Photographs: Mike Blum •

JADINE

NOTE: **T.** = tablespoon
tsp = teaspoon

EDITORIAL MANAGEMENT:
RAQUEL LÓPEZ VARELA

EDITORIAL COORDINATION
ANTONIO MANILLA

RECIPES Y FOOD STYLING:
TATIANA COTO

PHOTOGRAPHS:
MIKE BLUM

CONTRIBUTORS:
HANS VENIER
ASDRÚBAL LEIVA

DESIGN:
MAITE RABANAL

LAYOUT:
MAITE RABANAL
JORGE GARRÁN MAREY

EDICIONES JADINE S.A.

www.edicionesjadine.com
E-MAIL: info@edicionesjadine.com
P. O. BOX: 13894-1000
SAN JOSÉ, COSTA RICA
CENTROAMÉRICA

© COMERCIALIZATION: EDICIONES JADINE S.A.
© RECIPES AND FOOD STYLING: TATIANA COTO
© PHOTOGRAPHS: MIKE BLUM
© EDITION & DESIGN: EDITORIAL EVEREST, S. A.
CARRETERA LEÓN-LA CORUÑA, KM 5 - LEÓN

ISBN: 84-241-0846-9
LEGAL DEPOSIT: LE: 1576 - 2005
PRINTED IN SPAIN - IMPRESO EN ESPAÑA

EDITORIAL EVERGRÁFICAS, S. L.
CARRETERA LEÓN-LA CORUÑA, KM 5
LEÓN (SPAIN)

www.everest.es
Customer Information Service: +34 902 123 400

!The Flavors of Costa Rica!

Mmmm… Sometimes it tastes like cool rain on a tropical forest… like the sun, sand and sea… like fresh fruits… the city… the mountains… How can such a small country be so rich in such diverse flavors?

You could say that Costa Rica is like an "Olla de Carne", many types of vegetables mixed with beef drenched in an exquisite broth, cooked over a low flame. There is such a variety of people, geography, climates, and animals all surrounded by an exuberant natural environment: Like an "Olla de Carne", many types of vegetables mixed with beef drenched in an exquisite sauce, cooked over a low flame.

That must be why "Ticos" are so full of flavor. Our people savor joy, savor closeness, cheer, fun and, since "variety is the spice of life", you could say that Costa Rica is a grand menu to be enjoyed.

Sometimes our country tastes like the green of the lush vegetation that surrounds us: mountains, plains, and tropical forests. The rain transforms the green, making it more intense, deeper, and at those times, there is nothing better than a good cup of coffee, a tortilla with cheese and warm conversation.

Sometimes our country is served hot as it is on the Pacific beaches where a good "ceviche", and an ice-cold horchata drink, all enjoyed under the shade of a palm tree by the sea, turns it into a refreshing and incomparable recipe.

There are times when the taste of Costa Rica is garnished with a trip to the countryside, a dip in a stream, horseback riding in the mountains -refried beans on tortilla-, "picadillo", pasta and tuna salad, or even chicken with rice.

At times, the country tastes more like a city: cars going from here to there, people working, the multi-flavored "casados" and-red hot "chileros". We love hot, spicy food; in fact, you could say that we Ticos are very spicy, and things heat up even more at night. The dance floors, the discos, and community fiestas are a tangy sampling of the Tico flavor, at its zesty best. Nothing goes bettter with those specials moments than "bocas" of fried cassava, pork and garbanzo beans, patacones and, why not, a hearty session of salsa or merengue.

Besides the flavors associated with certain places and climates, occasionally the country is filled with seasonal flavors, and then you can delight in creations such as the "pejibaye" cream soup during the October rains, mango ice cream during Holy Week, eggnog at Christmastime, and warm hugs. We Ticos love the warmth of human contact, the heat of the sun, the fervor of our dishes, but above all, the warmth of our Costa Rica.

Our country can be a delight to savor, but you have to try it to discover it.

This book brings together the work of two professionals whose goal is to attest to the variety of Tico flavors, so that you might dare to prepare, and to enjoy, the rich essence of Costa Rica.

Bon Appétit!

BEVERAGES

Egg Nog (Rompope)

**1.4-1.9 LITERS
(6-8 CUPS)**
INGREDIENTS

1 liter (4 1/3 cups) **milk**
3 beaten **egg yolks**
230 grams (1 cup) sugar
1 T. **cornstarch**
0.050 liters (1/4 cup)
water
2 sticks **cinnamon**
0.250 liters (1 cup) **dark
rum** or **cognac**
1/4 tsp **Vanilla**

1. Sterilize the bottles to be used for the eggnog. Before filling the bottles rinse with a little rum or cognac.

2. Heat the milk together with the sugar and cinnamon. When the mixture starts to boil add the cornstarch dissolved in water, remove from heat and strain.

3. Add the beaten egg yolks and return to heat stirring constantly (do not let it boil).

4. Let cool stirring periodically. When the mixture has completely cooled, add the rum and pour into bottles.

5. Refrigerate and serve chilled.

Fruit Drinks

INGREDIENTS

One of the following **peeled, diced fruit**: pineapple, papaya, star fruit (carambola), mango, melon, watermelon, blackberries, strawberries, etc.
Water
Sugar and **honey** to sweeten

1. Process fruit in blender.

2. Strain (optional).

3. Add water, sugar and honey to taste.

4. Serve with ice.

You may also combine two or more different fruits of your choice.
If you use citrics (oranges, lemons, etc.) squeeze the juice, and follow the same procedure starting at step 2.

"Horchata"

1.2 LITERS (5 CUPS)
INGREDIENTS

230 grams (1 cup) **rice**
230 gram (1 cup) shelled
peanuts (cleaned)
1 T. **ground cinnamon**
0.680 liters (3cups) **wate**r
Milk, vanilla, sugar to taste

1. Let the rice sit over night in 3 cups (0.680 liters) of water.

2. Process the rice in the blender with the peanuts and add milk and cinnamon to taste.

3. Serve chilled.

"Slippery" drink (Resbaladera)

2 1/3 LITERS (10 CUPS)
INGREDIENTS

230 grams (1 cup) **rice**
1/2 tsp **vanilla**
0.450 liters (2 cups)
water
2 T. **barleycorns**
2 liters (8 cups) **milk**
2 sticks **cinnamon**
1/8 T. **nutmeg**
Sugar to taste
Cola syrup to taste

1. Cook the rice, cinnamon, barley and nutmeg in water until the rice is ready. Make sure it doesn't stick to the pan.

2. Cool and process in the blender with a little milk.

3. Strain (fine).

4. Add the rest of the milk, the vanilla, sugar, and syrup to taste.

APPETIZERS

Shell macaroni and tuna salad

4-6 SERVINGS
INGREDIENTS

680 grams (3 cups) **pasta shells**
230 grams (1 cup) **tuna in oil**
230 grams (1 cup) **mayonnaise**
230 grams (1 cup) **peas** (canned)
2 T. **cilantro,** finely chopped
1 medium **onion,** finely chopped
1 T. **celery,** finely chopped
3 T. **lemon juice**
1 T. **mustard**
1 T. **vegetable oil**
Salt to taste

1. Cook the shells in water with oil and a little salt. Once cooked, drain and rinse with cold water.

2. In a large bowl mix all the ingredients together. You may garnish with fresh lettuce leaves and tomato before serving.

This salad can be served as a side dish with any lunch or dinner entrée.

"Tortillas" and refried beans

INGREDIENTS

2 cups **seasoned beans** (See recipe on page 85)
1 T. **oil**
1/2 stick **margarine**
Tomato, peeled, seeded, grated

FRIED TORTILLAS
8-12 **corn tortilllas**
Vegetable oil

1. Process the beans in the blender until they are totally puréed.

2. In a large skilled melt the margarine with the oil. Pour the beans in and stir so they won't stick.

3. Check the seasoning. If you wish you can add more Worcester-shire sauce and/or salt.

4. Cut the tortillas into quarters. Fry in hot oil in a skillet. When they are golden brown take them out annd drain on paper towels before serving. Add salt and serve with the beans.

To make beans thinner, add cooked bean broth or grated tomato. To thicken, let them dry for a longer period on low heat, stirring constantly.

"Patacones"

6 SERVINGS
INGREDIENTS

3 green **plantains**
Salt to taste
Vegetable oil

1. Cut the plantains into 3 parts; peel with a knife.

2. Cut into 1 inch (2.5 cm) rounds.

3. Lightly fry in very hot oil, remove and gently flatten each slice (you can use the bottom of a glass), fry again until golden brown.

4. Sprinkle with salt as soon as they are off the stove.

"Patacones" may be served as a first course or as an appetizer. They are usually served with refried beans and/or guacamole. They may also be part of the main dish.

"Ceviche"

4-6 SERVINGS
INGREDIENTS

1/2 kg (1 lb.) **Sea bass**
filleted and diced
(deboned)
2 T. **celery**, finely chopped
3 T. **cilantro**, finely
chopped
1/2 T. **parsley**, finely
chopped
1 large **onion**, finely
chopped
1 **bell pepper**, finely
chopped
6-8 **lemons**
0.110 liters (1/2 cup) **white**
vinegar
3 bay leaves
Vegetable oil, pepper
Salt to taste

1. Place the fish in a glass bowl with all other ingredients. The fish should be completely covered by the liquid.

2. Cover and marinade overnight in the refrigerator.

3. Serve cold with Russian dressing, tomato sauce or hot sauce as well as saltine crackers, "patacones" (fried green plantains) and/or avocado.

Cream of pejibaye

6-8 SERVINGS
INGREDIENTS

18 **pejibayes** (cooked, peeled and very finely chopped)
1.4 liters (6 cups) **chicken broth**
0.450 liters (2 cups) **heavy/double cream**
0.060 liters (1/4 cup) **butter** or **margarine**
4 T. **flour**
2 **onions,** diced
3 **bay** leaves
Salt and **pepper** to taste

1. Melt the butter or margarine and sauté the onion.

2. Stir in the flour little by little and then add the chicken broth, bay leaves, salt and pepper.

3. Process the pejibayes in the blender together with this mixture, return to pan and cook at medium heat for approximately 20 minutes, stirring constantly. Add the pejibaye and stir constantly for 20 minutes.

4. Turn down the heat and then add the heavy/double cream.

5. Add salt and pepper to taste.

Fried cassava

8 SERVINGS
INGREDIENTS

2 kilos (4.4 lbs) **cassava**
peeled and cut into medium
size pieces
1 head of **garlic**, peeled and
diced
2 **stalks** celery, diced
Salt to taste
Vegetable oil

1. Place the cassava in a pan along with the garlic, celery and salt. Cover with water and cook until the cassava is tender..

2. Once the cassava is tender (not mushy), drain and fry in very hot oil until golden brown.

3. Add more salt, if needed and serve immediately.

4. If you wish to serve it with a dipping sauce, mix mayonnaise with ketchup or make a dressing of olive oil with finely chopped garlic and parsley.

Tico salad

4-6 SERVINGS
INGREDIENTS

1 rinsed **lettuce**
230 grams (1 cup) **red
cabbage** finely sliced
1 **red onion,** cut into
rings
1 sliced **bell pepper**
2 grated **carrots**
1 **beet,** cooked and
diced
1 **avocado**

1. Tear the lettuce into pieces by hand (For best flavor, do not use a knife).

2. Combine the vegetables and toss with lemon juice, salt and/or your favorite dressing.

MAIN COURSES

Beef and vegetable stew (Olla de carne)

8-10 SERVINGS
INGREDIENTS

450 grams (1 lb.) **beef ribs**
680 grams (1 1/2 lbs.) **beef brisket**
1 **onion,** chopped
1 **bell pepper,** chopped
2 **stalks celery,** chopped
230 grams (1 cup) **cilantro,** chopped
1 head of **garlic,** chopped
1 T. **oregano,** dried
1 T. **thyme,** dried, **salt** to taste

VEGETABLES

1 young **chayote** (mirlinton)
3 **potatoes,** 2 **carrots**
2 **sweet potatoes**
2 ears of **corn,** white and/or yellow
450 grams (2 cups) **cassava**
3 **"guineos"** (smaller species of plantain)
1 **green plantain**
230 grams (1 cup) **squash,** well ripened

1. Cook all the ingredients together (except the vegetables) in a pressure cooker on high. Cook for 30 minutes after the cooker starts to steam and lower the heat.

2. Peel and chop the vegetables into pieces. Cook the vegetables together in salted water until tender, except the chayote and squash.

3. Mix the meat with all of the vegetables and continue to cook until all the ingredients are tender.

Mirliton (Chayote) and sweet corn "Picadillo"

4-6 SERVINGS
INGREDIENTS

2 young **chayotes** (mirliton) peeled and diced
3 ears of **corn,** white or yellow
2 diced **onions**
2 diced **bell peppers**
5 cloves diced **garlic**
1 stalk diced **celery**
110 grams (1 cup) chopped **cilantro**
230 grams (1/2 lb.) **pork loin,** cut into pieces
1/2 tsp **turmeric** or **annatto** (optional)
Salt, pepper and **ground cumin** to taste
Vegetable oil

1. Sauté an onion and a bell pepper, 1/2 cup (110 grams) cilantro, the garlic and celery. Add the pork, salt, pepper and cumin, and a little water. Cover and cook on low heat until tender.

2. In a separate pan, sauté the remaining vegetables, add the corn and cover. Let the corn soften a bit, then add the chayote and pork and rectify the seasonings. Cover and cook at medium low heat, stirring occasionally, until all ingredients are well done.

Pork and garbanzo beans

6-8 SERVINGS
INGREDIENTS

PORK
680 grams (1 1/2 lbs.) **pork loin** cut in small pieces
6 strips chopped **bacon**
2 **onions**, 1 **bell pepper**
170 grams(3/4 cup) **celery,** 5 cloves **garlic**
2 **tomatoes,** peeled, grated, and seeded
110 grams (1/2cup) **cilantro**
1 tsp **thyme**, dried
1 tsp **oregano**, dried
Salt to taste, **vegetable oil**

GARBANZO BEANS
680 grams (3 cups) **garbanzo beans**, uncooked
1 **onion**, 1 **bell pepper**
110 grams (1/2 cup) **celery**
4 cloves **garlic**, 110 grams (1/2 cup) **cilantro**
Salt to taste

1. Fry the bacon with a little oil in a large frying pan on medium heat. When the fat has melted, add the chopped onion, peppers, and celery. Sauté until tender. Add the chopped garlic and the meat, followed by the tomatoes, thyme, salt and cilantro. Cover and cook on low heat until the meat is completely tender.

2. Let the garbanzo beans stand in water overnight. The next day, drain and cook in pressure cooker with all the ingredients. Add enough water to cover the garbanzos by 3.5 cm (1 1/2 inches). Cook on high, and continue cooking for 20 minutes after the cooker starts to steam.

3. Mix with the pork and boil for another 10 minutes.

Cassava pie

6 SERVINGS
INGREDIENTS

2 kg (4.4 lbs) **cassava,** peeled and
cut into medium size squares
450 grams (1 lb.) **pork loin,**
ground
4 **eggs**
110 grams (1/2cup) **young cheese,**
grated
3 T. **margarine**
1 **onion,** finely chopped
1 **bell pepper,** finely chopped
1 stal **celery**
2 **tomatoes,** peeled, chopped,
remove seeds
6 clove **garlic,** chopped
Salt and **pepper** to taste
Vegetable oil

1. Cook the cassava in salted water, once it is soft mash it. Add margarine, cheese and 2 whole eggs, plus one egg white.

2. Sauté the onion, bell pepper, celery and garlic. Add meat, tomatoes, one chopped hard-boiled egg, salt and pepper.

3. Smooth half of the cassava mixture over the bottom of a greased pan. Next add the meat, and finally the remaining half of the cassava. Brush the top with remaining egg yolk and sprinkle with grated cheese.

4. Place in oven until golden brown.

Chicken and rice

6-8 SERVINGS
INGREDIENTS

2 **chicken breasts,** filleted, skinned
4 **chicken legs,** filleted, skinned
1 tsp **thyme,** dried, 1 tsp **oregano,** dried
450 grams (2 cups) **rice**
230 gram (1 cup) **peas**
2 large **tomatoes,** peeled, diced, and seeded,
2 **bell peppers,** diced, 2 stalks **celery,** diced
6 cloves **garlic,** diced
2 medium **onions,** diced
3 T. **margarine**
Salt and **pepper** to taste
Vegetable oil
Turmeric to taste (adds color to the rice)

1. Marinade the chicken in the dry herbs (thyme, oregano and salt) and a little oil for a few hours or, if possible, overnight.

2. Sauté one onion, one bell pepper, a stalk of celery, 3 garlic cloves and the tomatoes. Add the chicken pieces, pour in 0.110 liters (1/2 cup) water and cover. Cook until tender, stirring occasionally.

3. Cook the peas separately until slightly softened and save the water. Melt the margarine with a tablespoon of vegetable oil. Fry the remaining onion, bell pepper, celery, and 3 garlic cloves. Add the rice and fry for 5 more minutes.

4. Add the strained peas and chicken (with broth and seasonings it was cooked in). Pour 3 cups of liquid from the peas into the rice, if there is not enough liquid, use water. Once it starts to boil cover and cook on medium heat until the rice is done. Cook until dry or leave slightly moist, depending on your preference.

"Casado"

SERVES 1
INGREDIENTS

110 grams (1/2 cup) **white rice,** cooked (See recipe on page 84)

110 grams (1/2 cup) **beans,** cooked and seasoned (See recipe on page 85)

110 grams (1/2 cup) **"picadillo"** of your choice (See pages 34, 44, 50)

75 grams (1/3 cup) **heavenly plantains,** (See recipe on page 66)

Salad (See recipe on page 28)

Meat

1. You can choose your favorite meat. Common favorites include steak and onions, chicken in gravy, tongue in sauce, shredded or "pulled" meat, etc. The most traditional salad served with this meal is prepared with cabbage, carrots, and tomatoes with lemond juice and salt, and sometimes a dressing of mayonnaise and ketchup.

A "casado" basically includes rice, beans, plantains, some "picadillo" (hash), or even "barbudos", or macaroni (pasta), in some cases dipped in egg, some kind of meat and salad. Frequently "gallo pinto" is substituted for the rice and beans. Traditionally the "casado" is served at lunchtime, all together on the same plate.

String bean and carrot (Hash) "Picadillo"

4-6 SERVINGS
INGREDIENTS

680 grams (1 1/2 lbs) **string beans**
2 medium **carrots**
1 diced **onion**
1/2 diced **bell pepper**
170 grams (1/2 cup) chopped **cilantro**
2 cloves peeled and diced **garlic**
1 stalk diced **celery**
Salt to taste (approx. 1 T)
Vegetable oil

1. Wash and cut tips off the string beans, then cut into medium-sized pieces.

2. Peel and dice the carrots.

3. In a large pan, sauté the remaining ingredients in oil. Just before the onion softens, add the string beans and the carrots. Sauté for a bit longer. Cover and cook on medium low heat stirring occasionally, until the vegetables are tender.

This recipe does not include meat, wich makes it more like a stew. However, as in the hash recipes on pages 34 y 50, by following the instructions for those recipes, you can perfectly add the meat. For this particular hash, it is better to use a tender cut of beef.

"Barbudos"

5 SERVINGS
INGREDIENTS

30 **string beans** (rinse
and remove tips)
1 T. **flour**
0.075 liters (1/3 cup)
vegetable oil
2 **eggs**
Salt to taste

1. Cook the string beans in salted water until tender. Drain.

2. In a separate bowl, beat the egg whites until they form peaks;
add the yolks, the flour and the salt. Mix thoroughly.

3. Separate the string beans into groups of 6, dip into batter and
fry in hot oil in a frying pan.

"Gallo pinto"

2-3 servings

INGREDIENTS

340 grams (1 1/2 cups)
black beans, whole,
cooked the day before
(See recipe
on page 85)
450 grams (2 cups) **white
rice,** cooked (see recipe
page 84)
1 **onion**
1/2 **red bell pepper**
4 T. **cilantro**
3 cloves **garlic**
2 T. **Worcestershire sauce**
3 T. **margarine**
Vegetable oil
Salt to taste

1. Sauté the chopped onion with bell pepper in vegetable oil and margarine. When tender, add the chopped garlic. When the mixture starts to brown, add the beans and salt. Cook on medium heat for a while until some of the liquid evaporates.

2. Finally add the rice, previously prepared with cilantro, mix together and remove from heat. Cover and let stand for 5 minutes before serving.

This traditional meal is usually served for breakfast; however, it may be eaten at any of the three meals, and is basic fare at any of them. If served at breakfast, it is usually accompanied by eggs (scrambled or fried), bread, sour cream, fresh cheese and sausage. If served at lunch or dinner, it is generally part of a "casado" as a substitute for beans and rice.

Smoked pork sausage and potato "Picadillo"

4-6 servings
INGREDIENTS

500 grams (1 1/4 lbs)
potatoes, peeled and cut
into medium-sized
pieces
4 **chorizos**/or **hot
sausages**/or a
combination of the two
1 **onion,** diced
1 stalk diced **celery**
1 diced **red bell pepper**
2 T. chopped **cilantro**
3 cloves chopped **garlic**
Vegetable oil
Salt to taste

1. Cover potatoes with salted water and cook until soft. Drain.

2. In a separate pan, sauté the onions, bell peppers and celery in vegetable oil. When softened, add the garlic and the "chorizo". Using a wooden spoon, break up the "chorizo" until it crumbles. Cook on medium high until well done.

3. Add the potatoes and the cilantro, stirring constantly to avoid sticking. Lower the heat and let the potatoes continue to cook and absorb the flavor.

DRESSINGS AND CONDIMENTS

Marinated chiles

**MAKES 560 GRAMS
(2 1/2 CUPS)**
INGREDIENTS

6 **jalapeño peppers,** washed
1/2 medium **onion,** julienne
170 grams(3/4 cup)
chopped **cilantro** (optional)
0.060 liter (1/4 cup) white
vinegar
Juice of 5 **lemons**
Salt to taste

1. Cut some of the peppers into slices and/or halves. Leave the rest whole.

2. Mix all the ingredients and store in a covered glass container.

Onion vinaigrette

6-8 SERVINGS
INGREDIENTS

110 grams (1/2) cup **oil**
0.060 liter (1/2 cup)
white vinegar
0.060 liter (1/4 cup)
onion, diced
1/2 T. **oregano,** ground
Salt and **pepper** to
taste

1. Sauté the onions in oil until they start to turn golden brown.

2. Add the rest of the ingredients and cook until the onion changes color.

3. Let cool and refrigerate.

Vegetable marinade (Escabeche)

MAKES 2.8 LITERS / 12 CUPS
APPROXIMATELY
INGREDIENTS

4 **carrots** julienne
1 **cauliflower** separated into florets
340 grams (1 1/2 cups) **string beans,** cut into 2.5 cm (1 inch) pieces
2 **onions,** cut into rings
4 cloves **garlic,** crushed
1 **bell pepper,** cut into strips
2 tsps **salt**
0.075 liters (1/3 cup) **oil**
4 **cloves**
3 **bay** leaves
4 **oregano** leaves
0.340 liters (1 1/2 cups) **white vinegar**
0.450 liters (2 cups) **water**

1. Fry the garlic in oil and add 0.060 liter (1/4 cup) water and the carrots. Cook for 5 minutes.

2. Add the cauliflower and string beans. After 5 minutes add vinegar, remaining water, vegetables and all seasonings.

3. Cook on low heat for approximately 1 hour, until all the vegetables are tender.

4. Transfer to a jar or glass container and refrigerate.

DESSERTS

Rice pudding (Arroz con leche)

6 SERVINGS

INGREDIENTS

150 grams (2/3 cup) **rice**
1 liter (4 1/3 cups) **milk**
2 **egg yolks**
230 grams (1 cup) **sugar**
3 sticks **cinnamon**
Zest of half **lemon**
1 can sweetened **condensed milk**
Water
Raisins (optional)

1. Place the rice in a pan filled with water, let stand for approximately 2-3 hours.

2. Drain and measure liquid. Heat with the same amount of water, add cinnamon. Cover and cook on medium heat until done.

3. Add the milk, beaten egg yolks, sugar, lemon zest and raisins (optional).

4. Continue cooking on medium heat, stirring constantly until it starts to thicken. When the rice is cooked, add the condensed milk and stir for another 5 minutes. Serve hot or cold. Sprinkle with ground cinnamon.

Bean and plantain turnovers

12-15 SERVINGS
INGREDIENTS

6 ripe **plantains,** ends
removed and cut in half
lengthwise
340 grams (1 1/2 cups)
refried beans (See recipe
on page 85)
1 T. shortening of **lard**
340 grams (1 1/2 cups)
sugar
Ground **cinnamon,** to taste
Vegetable oil for frying

1. Cook the plantains with the peel still on in water and a cup of sugar.

2. When the plantains start to puff up and come out of the peel, remove from heat and drain. Peel and purée with the lard.

3. Form plantain batter into circles and fill with the refried beans, close over the beans. Fry the turnovers in hot oil, and sprinkle with sugar and cinnamon.

These turnovers can also be filled with cheese or with a combination of cheese and refried beans.

Heavenly plantains

8-10 SERVINGS
INGREDIENTS

110 grams (1/2 cup)
margarine
340 grams (1 1/2 cups)
sugar
1 tsp ground **cinnamon**
1/2 tsp ground **nutmeg**
1/4 tsp ground **cloves**
1 **lemon**
4-6 ripe **plantains**, cut
into thick slices
0.450 liters (2 cups)
water or enough to
cover plantains
Vanilla to taste

1. Place the margarine, 1 cup (230 grams) of sugar, cinnamon, nutmeg, cloves, lemon juice, vanilla and plantains in a frying pan. Fry until they start to turn a light golden brown.

2. Add water to cover, and sprinkle the remaining sugar on top.

3. Cover, lower heat and cook until all the liquid is gone and they are covered with caramel and they are caramelized.

Mango and coconut ice cream

6-8 SERVINGS
INGREDIENTS

450 grams (2 cups) **mango,** well-ripened
(puréed in blender and strained)
4 **egg yolks**
150 grams (2/3 cup) **powdered sugar,** sifted
1 T. **lemon juice**
110 grams(1/2 cup) **coconut cream**
110 grams (1/2 cup) **heavy cream**

1. Mix the puréed mango with lemon juice, coconut cream and heavy cream.

2. Using a double boiler, mix the egg yolks, sifted sugar and stir until thickened. Remove from heat and continue beating until it cools. Pour into the mango mix, a little at a time, stirring with a metal spoon.

3. Pour into a rectangular pan 4 1/3 cups (1 liter). Cover with aluminum foil and place in the freezer until completely frozen.

4. Scrape out of pan with a spoon and place in a food processor or blender. Process on high until softened.

5. Return to original pan and let stand in freezer overnight.

Coconut caramels

INGREDIENTS

2 grated **coconuts**
1,400 grams (6 cups) **brown sugar**
230 grams (1 cup) **water** or **milk**

1. Heat the sugar, with the water or milk, stirring constantly, until the mixture turns syrupy.

2. Add the coconut and continue stirring until it all gets sticky.

3. While still hot, spread on a cookie sheet or a board covered with waxed paper. Let cool and cut into squares.

COFFEE COOMPANIONS

Sweet corn pancakes (Chorreadas)

8-10 MEDIUM-SIZED
PANCAKES
INGREDIENTS

6 ears of **corn** on the cob
4 **eggs**
1/8 tsp **salt**
3 T **sugar**
Vegetable oil

1. Grate the corn to remove kernels and process in blender.

2. Mix with the other ingredients.

3. Pour a little oil into a Teflon frying pan and then spoon the batter into the pan. Turn the pancake over when it starts to turn a golden brown. They are normally eaten hot.

They are usually accompanied by salted fresh cheese and/or sour cream.

Banana cake

16 SERVINGS

INGREDIENTS

9 very ripe **bananas**
110 grams (1/2 cup) **margarine**
230 grams (1 cup) **sugar**
2 **eggs**
0. 230 liter (1 cup) **milk**
450 grams (2 cups) **flour**
4 T. **baking powder**
1 T. ground **cloves**
1 T ground **nutmeg**
1 tsp **vanilla**
230 grams (1 cup) **nuts**

1. Preheat oven to 180 °C (350 °F).

2. Mash the bananas together with the margarine and sugar.

3. In a separate bowl, sift the flour and the baking powder together.

4. Beat the eggs until light in color and foamy in texture and then add them to the banana purée, milk, and vanilla. Slowly add the dry ingredients. Cover the nuts with flour, and fold into the mixture.

5. Pour the batter into a greased loaf pan or bundt cake pan and bake at 180 °C (350 °F) for one hour. Cool for 20 minutes. Remove from pan and let cool completely before slicing.

Tortillas and cheese

10-12 SERVINGS (MEDIUM SIZE)
INGREDIENTS

560 grams (2 1/2 cups) white
corn **flour**
Water
Salt
230 grams (1 cup) **fresh cheese**
which melts easily, grated
Vegetable oil

1. Place the flour in a deep bowl, gradually add water while mixing with your hands (kneading), until batter is well mixed but not sticky.

2. Add the cheese and mix well.

3. Heat up a tortilla pan or frying pan, smooth oil over the surface using a napkin. When a drop of water on the pan continues to jump for a few seconds, the correct temperature has been reached.

4. Form into balls approximately 5 cm (2 inches). Place them between to pieces of waxed paper or cellophane, squash with a plate and continue to extend and form the tortilla as evenly as possible using your fingers, until you reach a thickness of 4 mm (1/8 inch).

5. Hold between your two outstretched hands and place in the pan, first the center and then the sides simultaneously (so no air will be trapped underneath). Cook for 1 minute and turn over. Check constantly until tiny golden brown spots begin to appear on the tortilla. Serve immediately.

Corn bread

12 SERVINGS
INGREDIENTS

170 grams (3/4 cup) **margarine**
6 ears of **corn** on the cob
300 grams (1 1/3 cups) **sugar**
150 grams (2/3 cup) **wheat flour**
1 T **baking powder**
4 **eggs**
700 grams (3 cups) **fresh cheese,**
grated
1/8 tsp **salt**

1. Grate the corn or remove kernels and process in blender.

2. Beat the eggs and add to grated corn.

3. In a separate pan, melt the margarine and mix in the flour, sugar and salt as well as the egg mixture. Add the grated cheese and baking powder.

4. Pour into a greased and floured baking pan and bake at 177 °C (350 °F) until golden brown (1 hour 20 minutes approx.).

BASIC RECIPES

White rice

MAKES 1.27 KG (5 CUPS)
INGREDIENTS

450 grams (2 cups)
washed rice
560 grams (3 cups)
hot water
1 **onion,** finely
chopped
1/2 **bell pepper,** finely
chopped
1 stalk **celery,** finely
chopped
5 cloves **garlic,** finely
chopped
3 T. **oil**
1 1/2 tsp **salt**

1. Heat the oil in a pan; add the onion, bell pepper, and the celery. When softened, add the garlic and continue cooking for another minute. Add the drained rice. Fry with the onion, pepper, celery and garlic until golden brown.

2. Add hot water and salt. Cover and let boil until all the water is absorbed.

3. When the rice is cooked, remove from heat and mix with a spoon. Cover and let stand a while longer.

> Rice is one of the most common side dishes or entrees in Costa Rican cooking. Frequently it is the main or only starch in a balanced meal, as in the case of the "casado". Rice is used in many other recipes such as "gallo pinto", chicken and rice, rice and garden vegetables, pork and rice, hearts of palm and rice, etc. In fact it is even used for desserts such as rice pudding and oven baked rice cake, etc.

Fresh tomato sauce

MAKES 900 GRAMS (4 CUPS)
INGREDIENTS

5 **tomatoes,** peeled and
grated, remove seeds
1 diced **onion**
1 stalk diced **celery**
5 cloves chopped **garlic**
3 **oregano** leaves
1 **bay** leaf
3 T. **oil**
1 1/2 tsp **salt**
3/4 ts **sugar**

1. In hot oil, sauté the onion, bell pepper and celery, cook a little and then add the garlic.

2. Add the tomatoes, and other ingredients, and cook for a while on medium heat.

3. If you prefer, you can process the sauce in a blender.

Beans

1. Let the beans soak in water over night. Drain and rinse.

2. Place in a pressure cooker together with all the ingredients, cover with water about 5 cm (2 inches).

3. Cook on high; once the cooker starts to steam, lower the heat and cook for 30 minutes.

INGREDIENTS
500 grams (2 1/2 cups) **beans**
2 **onions**, chopped
2 **red bell peppers**, diced
1 head of **garlic**, chopped
6 **oregano** leaves
2 **stalks** celery, finely chopped
170 grams (3/4 cup) **cilantro**, finely chopped
Water and **salt**

Seasoned beans

1. Melt the margarine with the oil. Add the onion, bell pepper and celery. Sautée until softened. Add the garlic, cilantro and tomato. Cook until the tomato evaporates a little.

2. Add the beans with very little liquid, Worcestershire sauce and salt, stirring occasionally so they won´t stick. Let them cook until the liquid evaporates.

3. You may mash the beans with a wooden spoon, against the sides of the pot or skillet, so they will thicken faster.

For this recipe you can use red or black beans; however, traditionally black beans are used more often. Cooked beans can be eaten as a black soup ("Sopa Negra") accompanied by hard-boiled eggs, cheese or even avocado. The Seasoned Bean recipe is part of the traditional "casado" or used to make "gallo pinto", and the refried beans are used in a number of recipes, either alone as an appetizer, as a companion dish for "patacones", or even as a stuffing for plantains. Beans are a staple in the Costa Rican diet and form the basis for many of its traditional dishes.

INGREDIENTS
4 1/2 CUPS

3 cups **cooked beans** (see recipe above)
2 chopped **onions**
1 **red bell pepper**, chopped
7 garlic **cloves**, chopped
1 **celery stalk**, finely chopped
3/4 cup **cilantro**, finely choppped
1 **tomato** peeled, seeded and grated
1/4 cup **margarine**
2 tsp **vegetable oil**
Worcestershire sauce and **salt**

Glossary

ACHIOTE: A natural red food coloring, an excellent source of vitamins, similar to páprika.

BARBUDOS: String beans dipped in an egg batter and fried.

BISTEC: A type of beef cut. Comes from the English word "beefsteak"

BOCA: Costa Rican word for appetizers.

CAJETA: Similar to caramels.

CARAMBOLA: Star fruit; a tropical fruit, good for making natural drinks.

CASADO: A midday meal in Costa Rica. A combination of rice, beans, cold slaw and some sort of meat or fish.

CHILERO: Hot pepper mixture.

CHORIZO: Pork Sausage.

CHORREADAS: Corn Pancakes.

GALLO: Costa Rican word for a small tortilla wrapped around a portion of sausage, cheese, mashed potatoes, or anything you wish to put in it.

GALLO PINTO: Traditional Costa Rican Breakfast: a combination of rice and beans and seasonings.

GUACAMOLE: Purée made from avocado.

GUINEO: Small type of green bananas.

JALAPEÑO: Type of hot pepper.

PATACONES: Green plantains, cut into rounds, mashed, then fried until crispy.

PEJIBAYE: A palm-sized fruit that looks like a miniature coconut.

PICADILLO Any combination of cooked meat and vegetables or a medley of cooked vegetables.

RESBALADERA: Traditional drink made from rice, with a "slippery" consistency.

SOPA NEGRA: A black bean soup served with a boiled egg.

TORTA: A flat cake or patty.

Index